Made in United States
North Haven, CT
08 March 2023

33768377R00057